A Lifestyle of Heaven Ascending

~

PAULA SARAHBONI MINGUCCI

Editor: Amy Drown

All rights Reserved
2016

A Lifestyle of Heaven Ascending
~

Ascending through Christ the Door
I dedicate this book to The Father, The Son Yeshua and Holy Spirit. They are my direct family members and my focus of all things. With love and gratitude I honor and thank them. Amen.

This book is about how to step into the kingdom of God.
We will go into hearing, sensing, and seeing as a prelude to ascending as a son. It's our position to take—to walk as a son—and understanding its reality on a daily basis. It's the journey and the lifestyle.

I had a dream on March 31, 2016. I saw a group of people who were unaware planning to go out into space. It was a mission beyond Mars. I felt they planned to go very far away. I felt concern in the dream as if they were in danger. The pope was sitting there, and I went to him and said, "They are planning a mission out into space." The pope said, "I know," and started to weep as if he was very sad about this. Kids kept coming up and interrupting us, so I would tell them, "I'll be with you in a minute." The second time I told the kids, "I'll be with you in a minute," I turned and saw the pope and the other men get into their cars. They were just shutting their car doors, as if I had missed the opportunity to keep talking to him about this. So I went back into the room and started to see this documentary on this very subject.

I saw how these luminaries were taking people's DNA
by going in through the nose. I watched like an x-ray image as they took parts of the DNA and broke them up as if they were harvesting them. When these beings, called luminaries, would go up to a person and get to their DNA through their nose, it killed them. I realized that these people going out in space were in grave danger. I was highly

concerned, and as I watched this, I felt these beings appear in the room and tried to come to me using a spirit upon the back of my head, in the mind area. I felt this coming onto me as if to take me over. I went into another room and shut the door. As I did this I put my hand on the back of my head and applied the blood of Jesus. And that spirit had left me.

In another scene in the dream, I was in a basement with stuffed animals like a child would have. I felt emotions for these stuffed animals and took one or two to bring upstairs with me. I felt sorry for the other ones whom I left behind, and yet they were talking and saying they were okay and would be here—or something to that affect—as if speaking to me and to one another. So there was the knowledge that these stuffed animals were "alive." When I woke up, I heard the word, "Nimrod," and that the spirits that died before the flood, or the half-people, half-angels, had bodies according to Enoch.

These spirits were looking for a body, and were partnering with these entitles from space, called the luminaries, in order to extract DNA to create bodies that they could inhabit. The stuffed animals had demonic spirits in them. That is why some people get a soul tie or feel connected to them. This I felt was just an example of what they did. A discerning person could see it. So these beings wanted to create a body they could inhabit from a different dimension, so they can come to the earth and inhabit it, possess it and take it over. And the Lord said, "That is why we need the order of Melchizedek." In this order, you ascend into heaven as a priest and king in order to become the oracle and legislator into the earth. These are the functions of the four faces of God. Jesus said in the prayer, "Thy will be done on earth as it is in heaven, thy kingdom come on earth as it is in heaven." Part of a king's M.O. is to gain and take over territory. This is not in a hostile way, but with the love and power of God in Christ.

Nimrod means, "he will revolt," and "he was in contempt of God." Nita Johnson had a dream of people playing in a shark-infested pool. They would fall in, and the water said, "I am tired of sitting here waiting; I'll make myself a big wave and take over the city of Zion."

3

And the Lord kept telling Nita, "Nita, come inside of me," and he kept repeating himself until she did after the third request, and she and the Lord were as one. That was the answer to her frantic appeal about the sharks.

What is the order of Melchizedek?

Four faces: Lion, Ox, Eagle Man, and the Yod Hey Vav Hey. These are the faces of the operation of God. Melchizedek had done his priestly duty this way. He was in heaven and then came to earth and walked among people as a priest and king. The king and priest function in heaven. As we ascend by faith into the Holy of Holies and stand before the Mercy seat of the Lord, we must understand the functions of each. A priest intercedes and ministers to the Lord. A king decrees what is to be so (using the word and getting mandates and scrolls from heaven). The oracle/prophet and apostle/legislator function on earth. The oracle will just speak the voice of God because they are in complete oneness. When I have ascended with others, many many times I have watched Jesus move his mouth, speaking the exact words that were coming out of mine.

Legislator is also one who makes decisions regarding situations and nations, such as putting up a boundary stone to say to the enemy that he cannot cross this line. For example, I've known people who live in difficult situations and have put a boundary stone up for a daughter or son, saying satan cannot take their life until they are fully serving God, and what is on their scroll is fulfilled. This happened once to someone who took their life by accident and came back: their heart stopped, but they came back and fully recovered because, it is believed, someone put up a boundary stone on their behalf.

When you ascend, you ascend as the priest first, going into the holy of Holies and ministering before the Lord. You intercede and worship God, praise and give him thanks. The king declares and decrees. These two function in heaven. You frame through your breath, words, or oracles, creating, as your words have power, you release decrees over nations and legislate what you had won in the courts through repentance. Courts again are done by faith. It's an ongoing function

4

that has many facets. Many of us are learning as we go. We have the basic platform and walk that out. Every day and every situation and every time it may be different one day from another. Those who can are able to get into groups and ascend together. Some of us are called to do that much like The Ladies of Gold by James Mahoney were called to gather. And along side of that is personal ascending and connecting with God. And with that is the transportation in the spirit, as God will take a person in their dreams or while awake, to do the work of the Lord.

So this book is to help you start your lifestyle of ascending.

~

ONE

Chapter 1:

Help Me See

Help me see. Help me perceive. Help me sense. Help me ascend.

We need to get quiet and still before the Lord to hear, see, perceive, sense, and ascend. I would like to thank all those who had gone before me to help pave the way. I always struggled to see. I started having visions and dreams after I fasted years ago, but then it faded in time because my pursuit of him faded. So it became less frequent until I began to pursue the Lord and more of the seeing gifts. I learned to pursue him and, as a result, the rest follows. So if you are one of those who want to see more, or want to see so that ascending may be a part of your journey, God will honor that by giving you layer upon layer, level upon level, going from glory to glory. The key is to not give up.

When the Lord wanted to blast me in the Holy Spirit He did so intensely that I was on the floor, laughing, hollering and was unable to walk or sit up for long. He first was giving me a little bit of his spirit, then a little bit more and wham. He hit me full tilt and down I went. So each time I was in his presence leading up to that final slam, he added a bit more.

In this book, it is my heart to help you on your journey to see, hear, sense and ascend, and to make it a lifestyle. God wants you there! I am writing this because I myself read books that helped me see. It was the way into this possibility. What you see, you can have, meaning that as you read, you can get impartations. So, Father, as they read through this, I pray the Holy Spirit gives them impartations into more of you in these ways. I ask you to land on everyone with the gifts of the spirit, those who read this and as they persevere as a son to grow in maturity you will add glory to glory. I speak this in Christ our heavenly bridegroom, for the one who steps into the four faces of God as a son.

Now more than ever God wants to communicate with you in visual form, not just through seeing, but through all senses. Before I go on, I want to acknowledge a few resources that I used in my journey. Did I suddenly "see" after I read these? No, but God honored my hunger in my pursuit and, as Paul Keith Davis once said, "I just fed my hunger." I think when you read these types of books, they will be a catalyst to bring you into this seeing realm. God honors hunger. And I did pray the prayers they offered. You may see differently than I do or they do, but that is okay. God doesn't make cookie-cutter Christians. We all have a unique part to play.

Some recommendations:
A book is by Michael Van Wyman, How to See in the Spirit, and The Veil by Blake Healy. I did two videos on THE REV group that helped many see and we are doing a third one shortly. The website www.theekklesiaofthemosthigh.com has content to help you grow. I have had many testimonies of people saying things like, "I have grown more in the last year than the 22 years of being a believer from being on your pages." Many had begun seeing where they never could before. Now remember, the enemy may throw everything at you including the kitchen sink to stop you. But that is only to give you strength. Sometimes when you are forced to run, your legs get stronger. When you are forced to fight, you become stronger.
So with that in mind, I write this book as an assignment from the Lord.

Let's start with a prayer
Dear Father, I am yours. I want to encounter you more as I walk this out with you. I want to see and perceive you more and as a result make it more enjoyable, edifying and profitable to see and sense things in the spirit. I am asking you to open my eyes and the other gates of my spirit, soul, and body to sense and perceive you more. Cleanse each of

my gates and renew my faith. Remove hindrances and blockages from my gateways that could hinder my perceptions. Father, I am asking you to cleanse and renew as I agree to sanctify myself to you and sanctify my eyes and all other gateways. Father, I don't want this for selfish reasons, but to be used for your glory, that I may walk in intimacy with you as well as help others. Use me as much as you possibly can and activate these gifts in me now as I lay down my own will and pick up yours. Give me the right motives to see and perceive, in Jesus' name. I step into your name, Jesus, and put you on and know you are in me and I am in you. Fill me up by the Holy Spirit in a new way and deposit the seven spirits of God in me so that I am fully functioning as a son and walking in maturity and right relationship with you now. In Jesus' name amen.

So I recommend the teaching "Gateways", the threefold nature of man by Ian Clayton (sonsofthunder) to walk through each gate. It does not have to be complicated. We do those by taking you by the hand to walk through each one on THE REV Facebook group. Go to this website to join: www.theekklesiaofthemosthigh.com

When we decide to sanctify ourselves unto God, we are setting ourselves apart. Many may not understand you, some may not want to hang out with you, and to be honest, the closer you get to the Lord, you often do not want to anyway, because their conversation ends up pulling you down. I have found in my own life that I could no longer tolerate talking to people about their day-to-day living. I would find myself anxious and I just wanted to talk about God. All other subjects became extremely boring to me. I was so intensely hungry, nothing else would do. I was incredibly passionate, and think that I still am. I mention this because it doesn't happen overnight, but rather as we run toward him and feed that passion, more comes.

In that decision that you have set yourself apart for him, even as you may study the order of Melchizedek, you will begin to care about what goes into your eye gates, what you listen to, what you watch and read. You have sanctified your gateways unto him, so purity is part of the protocol. Purifying yourself through repentance, through worship, through choosing to embrace the fire, choosing him along with repentance. As you choose to choose him and choose to not choose anything that would defile those gates, you become more purified. The more pure, the more power and the more authority one has. Kat Kerr has stated this as well.

Prayer

Father, open my eyes now to see what you are doing in the kingdom all around me. Purify my gateways. Father, I am asking you to activate everyone who just prayed that prayer. Amen.

Exercise

Close your eyes and say, Lord I step through your blood into the kingdom of heaven. Now in y0ur mind picture your closet. Turn on the light, and look around. Pull something off the shelf. Look at it. Put it back. Take something that is hanging up. Look at it, feel the texture of it. If you just did your laundry, does it have a scent of fabric softener? If not, pretend it does. Using your memory, you can smell that on your clothing. Your picture is no longer a picture, but a door. The door is the door of your spirit. Your spirit went to your closet. How did your spirit go there? The Holy Spirit is everywhere, and everywhere the Holy Spirit is, your spirit can go because it is made up of the same stuff. Not only that, but you can, as part of creator God, create using your memory. You can choose it and sanctify it through His blood. Once someone came from heaven and told their family member that they can eat things without it being put in their mouths. It is just put in their hand and goes right into their spirits. So when an angel tosses a chocolate chip cookie at me, I can taste it without it being put into my mouth. I see it and smell it and taste it.

Exercise:

Close your eyes. Think of another room, in the spirit walk into that room. Sit on a chair or a bed. Pick up a book, put that book down. If it has a lamp near by, turn on that lamp. Look up; there is a door, open that door above you to another realm. It looks like space, in your heart, through desire, fly through space and see an angel with you. Pass galaxies and nebulas all the way up into the kingdom of God into heaven. Step into a cloud that now has a floor of sapphire. Kneel before the throne of the Father and worship Him. Tell him the truth, that He is wonderful, awesome, beautiful, glorious and so on. Think of everything that you can that is good about the Lord. Pour out your heart. After you worship Him sit quietly and wait for Him to speak. Write down what you received. Do this exercise often.

Often when I am eating something like chocolate, in the spirit I toss some to all my angels and they say thank you. And they have what I am having. It's quite fun. Once I went in my car to a store and on the way I would pass restaurants, and when it was a pancake house, pancakes would end up on my windshield and if an ice-cream shop, an ice cream cone would end up slowly melting and running down the window. These angels were having a lot of fun that day. It was funny and I could see how they could just grab something from anywhere. That may be way out of your normal life, but it's a life and a reality I have been able to live in and you are able to as well. God wants us to live more in the supernatural, unseen world than this one because it is more real than this one. And as years go by, you will see there is a great purpose in all of this. We will need to walk through walls, and portal jump to avoid the UN and bring God glory and bring others into the kingdom. Some of us will be living more in space than on the earth. Actually like Enoch did. Be all there, not just in spirit. Enoch came back to the earth from time to time. These are the sons of God creation has been waiting for.

As you practice you will find that this is going to intensify, and before you know it, you will not only see, but smell and taste and you will be in an interactive state in heaven itself. Really there! Not just a picture, but there. Your spirit is attached to your body but can leave it. You can be in two places at once. There and here. The more you are there; the more you are unaware of your body.

TWO

Chapter 2:
Help Me Perceive

So Dear Reader, Jesus wants you to see, and perceive. I ask Holy Spirit to fill you up right now as you read this. It takes the Holy Spirit to sense and see. You have a spirit but Holy Spirit is a great friend and teacher, as the word says. Just as the word says to ask and you will receive. Do not let fear stand in your way. Fear is a spirit. It is your enemy. Open the door and kick him out.

Prayer:
I take authority over the spirit of fear and command it to go now, in Jesus' name. You have no place here. Jesus did not give me a spirit of fear, but of power, love and a sound mind. Amen.

So here is how I want you to think from now on. First, when perceiving, you may sense something. Feel something. God's spirit is communicating with you. Pay attention to everything.

Prayer:
Father, make me sensitive to anything you are doing, either by Holy Spirit or the angels. Thank you that as you open my eyes to see, you open my perception to sense. Sensing their presence, their movement and knowing what they are doing and when. In Jesus' name, amen. Father, I am asking you to activate everyone who just prayed that prayer. Amen.

Here are some things you may expect: Angel wings brooding over you; a wisp against your ear; a hand on your shoulder; waking up to angels singing; a picture, a word; being woken up for a reason; dreams; hearing God's voice; flashes of light near your eyes or in your room. God will respond to faith. Seek and you will find. Seeking takes faith. Are you seeking him and all that has to do with his kingdom on earth and in heaven? There is a stairway to heaven with your name on it!

When a person is taught to prophesy they are positioning themselves to do so. It's like when you get ready to catch a ball, you position yourself to catch it. So likewise you position yourself to prophesy. When we practice this, we go with the first thing that comes to our mind and you would need to just go with that. You don't second-guess it. When you position yourself to see or sense, God sees you are putting your arms out to catch that ball. So then, since you have decided to catch the ball and you bring yourself into that position, you are ready to do so and God can and therefore does throw that ball to you. In the same way, position yourself mentally and in your heart to hear, see, sense, and perceive. And as a result of that position, you go with the first thing that pops into your mind.

Try this: Sit quietly and say, "Father, I love you," and sit and wait and expect a response. He always says, "I love you, too." Do that every day. Say, "I love you, Lord," and wait for a response. The idea is to expect a response and wait to hear it. First thing that pops into your mind. If you have evil coming at you, you need to stop and get deliverance. Do bloodline cleansing. Repentance book by Natasha Vermaak Grbich.

DNA cleansing sessions,
DNA holds a record of everything both parents had done. We can get that cleaned up through repentance. Removing triggers and issues from our genetics. Jesus is in this very much, since I had read of an encounter of a young girl that the Lord came to and offered that explanation of satan putting negatives we must deal with on our DNA. That is why Jesus was able to transfigure, because He had pure DNA and pure DNA is light. Creative light. So it is important to stay in repentance and if you need help with specific needs that are relevant to you personally, I offer that here. God always gives me words for the people I minister to as well to help catapult you into your destiny. http://www.theekklesiaofthemosthigh.com/dnabloodline.html

THREE

Chapter 3:
The Lifestyle of Becoming

The Lifestyle of becoming is a life process. It includes repentance, and preparation and positioning. It takes time, and love and desire. It is something that God has to cultivate in you. We can ask the Lord to help us move into becoming one with Him. We can ask Him to direct our steps. We can ask Him to tether us to His purposes and bring His will into our hearts. We can also ask him to accelerate the process. Once I was in church and I got a word from the Lord. Are you going to take this seriously now? I thought I was taking it seriously. I sense learned that we can run after the relationship and the acquiring and at the same time, avoiding the Lord. We run from things we are afraid of. We need to trust Him when this is sensed in our hearts. The Lord is saying, do the best you can, be serious, be genuine and with things that you have no power over, hand them over to me. Let me do what I need to do, just obey. I tell you what, there is nothing like seeing the Father on the mountain with his glowing eyes of glory, and seeing and knowing Him and learning from Him. He has a personality, a power, a love, and a cleverness that is beyond expression. There is NOTHING like a relationship with the Father and His son Yeshua. It is the most awesome journey you will ever take on earth. This world is boring in contrast. One thing I wonder is how it is that anyone can live this life and be happy just in the flesh. He transforms us. I see this change, by time with Him and with worship toward Him, in purposeful pursuit. Its not just getting 'there' but it's the walk along the way that is awesome.

One thing that bugs me sometimes, (with due respect to all God's vessels in use for his glory of course) is when we the body say things like, "the glory or the blood or the gifts," and we remove the person which they are from. It's like concentrating on the gift and not the giver. So remember to always consider the person of the Lord Jesus Christ, and not separate out anything from him and focus on that only, like the glory or the blood. How about saying, "the blood of Jesus" or "the glory of God," or "the gifts of the Father, the gift of Holy Spirit." We can get disconnected from the head, as the word says, who is the ruler, father, friend, brother, king, and emperor of the universe. Like a child who grabs the gift out of the hand of the parent and runs away without even looking at the mom or dad whom the gift is from. No hello, no kiss, no I love you… some would call that an inconsiderate and spoiled child who takes his parents' love for granted, for it is not love that takes the gift out of their hand but selfishness without the acknowledging. Same with the word of God. The scriptures can become an idol as if the word was cut off from the source and we worship and think of just the scriptures and not the person of God. The author is a person whom we barely know if we just use the scriptures. One minister wisely said, "If I read a book about a person, that doesn't mean I know them personally." So the word is an introduction to the person. So much of our getting to know God is one-on-one with the author of the Bible as we seek him the person. The word does stay in our hearts if we read it but don't seek more of the scriptures by seeking him. Seek the more of God, like a well that is bottomless, and go deeper into himself using the word as a spring board or a diving board. We must jump, fly in mid-air and direct ourselves into that pool and once we ascend into it, swim into the deep. Deep cries out to deep. The deep of our souls and spirits and hearts cries out to the deep of God. The vast and limitless Father, creator, ruler and friend. Seek to know and love the person of God, what an awesome God he is and awesome personality he carries.

Regarding the Walk

It's important to not be constantly tuning your ears on purpose to the spirit world. This is unhealthy. Be open if it comes, but don't be looking for something to listen for. If so we can cause problems. If you are asking a question to give a word or doing ministry and you are ready for that, you should be safe. With that said, a question may come, "Can this be the enemy?" Well, if you have demons, yes. Or if the enemy is around because of open doors in your life, then yes. The familiars must be dealt with. They sound like your own voice.

But if you are repenting and cleansing your DNA and gateways, and you are asking for angels around you, let that thought go of it being the enemy. It's important as you dedicate your life and cleanse your bloodline through repentance. Be patient. Walk it out as well as pursuing the gifts at the same time. God wants you to sprinkle in the fun.

What is an open door? An open door is when you do something like watch horror movies, and then wonder why you have nightmares, or evil things you watch on TV, or music with immoral words in it. Even things like a sin such as a lie, gossip, quarreling, etc. How do I shut the door? Repent for the sin and for opening that door. Then close that door by saying, "I shut that door now, in Jesus' name." Do not reopen the door. When we repent, let's repent for our generational line and say we divorce ourselves from that trading floor which it came from. Sometimes your enemy may attack you if another person who lives with you listens to the garbage or watches it.

What do I do with demons that attack me? Picture the demon, even if you can't see it. Picture it by using your will and imagination, take it by the neck, and by faith step into the courts of heaven and as you walk in, say, "Father, what legal right does this have to attack me?" Even if you get a list of things that you never did, repent for each one. Say, "Father, I repent for… 1, 2, 3. I divorce myself from the trading floor in which it was founded on and ask for divorce papers. Thank you, Father." Then if you feel it still attacking you, recognize you may be dealing with several of these. Picture in your mind taking the second demon to court and doing the same thing, and the third demon you bring in and repeat that procedure. Soon you will feel the atmosphere clear. Once I had this happen, the atmosphere around me cleared up. The person who brought them in, when I went near them, I could feel the enemy around them, but it wasn't attacking me anymore. We need to teach people how to be free and stay free. So that is very simple. What we can struggle with familiar spirits that we must eventually over come to the point they give up and no longer hang around you. A familiar spirit sounds like you, your own voice, or perhaps a family member—that is why they call it familiar—and they can feel ingrained into your own thinking.

Fear is a spirit. You can command that spirit of fear to leave. Keep commanding it to leave. If it has a legal right, repent renounce and apply the blood of Jesus. By doing that you are saying, "No, I am not going to put my arm around you and walk through life with you as if you were my friend, because you are not." Separate yourself from defiling, unclean, impure things and thoughts, as if you need to dislodge it from your soul in rejection of it. If you are attacked with a thought that even shocks you, apply the blood of Jesus to that thought, repenting for opening that door. Sometimes we get attacked with other people's junk. If that is the case, do the same as if it were your own.

Dedicate yourself to God. If you are serious about God and serious about your relationship with God, he will help you and pave the way. If you take him seriously, he will take you seriously, so guard your heart, and also examine your heart. Examine your motives. Are they pure? Are you playing around or are you serious? If you are truly serious about God, you will want to dedicate yourself to him for his purposes and plans. Lay yourself down on the altar. You can use your imagination to do this. You are letting go of yourself and trading it for Him. That doesn't make you a robot, but it brings you into co-laboring, co-partnering and co-union, friendship, loyalty, faithfulness, covenant, love, purpose and support of heaven itself. Amen?

So when you pray and dedicate all your gateways to God and clean them up, you are making the pipeline so clear that the clean (Holy Spirit) water can flow through you. The cleaner you are the better. So don't stop doing that. If you get weary of it and overwhelmed, stop, and come back to it again sometime after a rest. Don't get weary. Keep going, it makes a **huge** difference. Sometimes the Lord will take you on a time travel to do this. For example, I had been taken back to the

Renaissance period in a dream. There were shiny silver knights near and my family member was a king. He and his wife were having marital problems and as I saw what went on, I woke up and repented for what they did and said. This was on my DNA as a result. I had no idea that they were in my family line until then. Other times, I was taken back during years of my mother I had not known. I saw her stuff, the struggles she went through and as a result got a list of things to repent and renounce. So ask God for those dreams to clue you in on what to repent for. When we are doing this, we are saying to God, I do not want any part of this on me or in me, and I agree with you and dislodge this from my soul. I crave you and your purity. So again, it's important to take stock of what you do. Jesus said to strive to enter the narrow gate. Strive, He said. So stop the movies and the music and the TV that are not pure. It is worth it to stop. R is completely out. PG-13 extremely rare if not never. Personally I can't stand music that doesn't have Holy Spirit on it, or having whack on it, like Justin Abraham says. So if it isn't got no whack on it, skip it. We will often see visions of the movie after we watch it. I heard others say this too. If I am bothered, I ask the Lord to wash it from my mind. You may even have a good reason to watch it. Sometimes God wants me to see something for a specific reason.

Images can be pollution and even some wall feeds on Facebook can be as Christian people you "friend" can sometimes be defiling. Not everyone who says they are truly are believers. A believer not just believes His existed, and died, but it is also believing what Jesus said, and if they did believe it then they would walk that out in their lives. We are all at different places, but some people are even stubborn and will not grow beyond babyhood. It's a choice to walk the narrow road, to strive toward that. What joy there is in doing so! It's also important to realize that images have a frequency. I like how Neville Johnson said that he deals with these accidental visuals by asking the Lord to come and wash it out of his mind. He then sees an angel washing him. So I often use this myself. It works.

While doing an event on The Rev, I was seeking the Lord on DNA cleansing since we were going to go to court for our autosomes. The

Lord showed me that when a person sins, their DNA frequency goes down, produces a dark spot and is passed down for the enemy to mess with us in that weak place. So we can change that through repentance, then words we speak in blessings. All words have a power to them, where God created through the word, frequency framing them up, using the original Hebrew living letters. In the same way, sentences like, "I know you are always sad, you always feel alone," are like word curses. You can end up agreeing with that statement and then inviting that curse into your life. Break out of it. Say, "Father I repent and renounce any word curse I came into agreement with and gave the enemy legal right." The Lord showed me that even if an actor acts a part of a villain, they are agreeing with that character in that act. So maybe the higher level of understanding can be caught here. So Father I bless my soul, body and spirit with words of life and affirmation. In Jesus' name.

I know that this walk of closeness to God is a choice. Some may not be able to handle it and, if that is the case, you don't have to. But some want to. He invites you to it, and it will matter later when you are in heaven. We are going to the level of heaven in which we belong. Some will not go make it into the holy of holies as a result.

Cleaning out the heart and the mind by repentance and replacing will help your mouth follow. The word says to renew your mind using his word. So we need to renew, reframe, replace. Positive thinking! If you take a glass of Diet Coke and a glass of water, and start to pour water into the glass of Diet Coke, eventually the coke will be 100% water. It is replaced. So can your soul, body, spirit, mind, and heart be renovated. Yes, even 100%. Start pouring in the good and it will displace the other stuff. Even regarding distractions.
I wake up with hearing angels singing a line to commune with me something, and then another or they give me pictures and speak to be daily. That is because I run after this with my whole heart. That means, I run after Him. His kingdom is awesome! What fun! I had never been so happy! We can have a big beautiful home with all we desired, but be lonely miserable sad and in despair. The inner life of the "kingdom within you" is what is true joy. The river of life never runs dry!

Taking communion is a good way to do that as well, so long as you think about his sacrifice, His blood, His body. I always think about Jesus' body and blood, replacing mine as I take it. His body and blood were sinless. So let His body and His blood, displace your body and your blood. I think about his body on the cross-crucified. I honor him. If you honor him, he will honor you.

About communion:

Some use anything for elements. I personally think we should use as close to the real thing as possible to represent his body and blood. Did you know that his blood had 24 chromosomes and one was from the Heavenly Father while the others where from his mother? I learned through a well known man of God from India, now in heaven, that Jesus looks like his mother. So he had taken on her likeness, and the flesh was created from her DNA and his dad's side was just one X chromosome, which explains that he was definitely part human and part God. When they put his blood under a microscope, which they found at the site of his crucifixion (the blood dripped down into the rock and into the container and onto the actual mercy seat, according to http://wyattmuseum.com , they took a sample of his blood. It was put under a microscope where you can see movement of life in the blood. It was explained that no one's blood dies. Little lights moving around under the microscope showed the light particles alive. The blood has the memory of all the things that happened in Jesus' time on earth, so we are taking that into ourselves which is eternal by the breath of God as well as all he did on earth. Donor transplant recipients suddenly find that they want to do things they didn't care to do before. Their lifestyle changes, their taste in music, or any thing else changes and becomes like the person who donated the organ. So you can expect that, as you take the body and blood of Jesus, your lifestyle will change and become like the recipient, who cast out demons healed the sick and walked on water. We become like Him.

The sound of matter

Once, after I felt I was wasting time going through a Facebook wall feed (not private groups that have gatekeepers, but wall feed) and some Christian YouTube videos, I repented for wasting time and feeling yuck from it. My angel said, as I was given a picture of the light going into my eyes, that these have a certain frequency that affect you. I am more than happy to go through the narrowest possible road he wills for me, because the rewards are so great. So the Lord is calling you to the sweet place of intimacy that few find.

I saw once while I was in a movie theater, many years ago, a demon standing in the front, looking at the people as the movie played. He looked as if he was looking for something. The Holy Spirit gave me the inspiration that he was looking to see if there is anything he can add into any one of these people. Attach something that is connected to what they already have. That is how strongholds are built. A stronghold is like a wall, sometimes two walls of defense that hold a king in a castle. That king is, in this case reference, an evil king. Repentance again, tears down the wall of defenses and as a result that demon king can be cast out.

A Key

God adds to you, the devil tries to subtract from you. Remember Jesus said the enemy wants to steal, kill and destroy. So that is a negative and subtracts from your life, and the scriptures tell us, whatsoever things are lovely, good, and of good report (nurturing and positive), to think on these things. They are a plus sign and add to your life. Anything that is not perfect is because of sin. No matter what, it will be traced back to a sin. All illness's, are a result of sin. The more light we have because of cleaning up, the more we will be able to transfigure as Jesus who had perfect DNA.

Matter having frequency it has also memory. The memory is stored. If an item is used for good it rejoices in that; if it is evil that item is grieved. When we sing and worship God out in creation, the creation actually feels like it is getting healed. I had an experience of this. Some have said the stars will turn and look at you. Likewise if you go out into nature and worship God in spirit and it truth, nature will look at you.

Put on Christ. He is pure, as if you were to see pure white light or pure light with pure colors like crystal colors of light. It is beautiful with the sound, frequency and vibration of heaven. Sinless, spotless and magnificent. Holy, like a large beautiful chandelier made of diamonds in the sun. That is where our souls need to be pure and all our gates clean. Then you will see God. The pure in heart will see God because it is in the heart that you see. Your heart has eyes. Purity is without darkness, sewage and slime or soot. It is crystal pure clean. You begin to gravitate toward this purity and clean clear holiness more and more. As you do, you can spot darkness easily. It can't hide; it's just there. Exposed. Then what? You can leave it or deal with it, depending on the situation. Angels want to be around that purity and love to worship God, and so they also don't like being around the dirt. So are you that same way?

Regarding warfare, Jesus fought it when Peter said, "No, Lord, that will not happen to you," regarding his word about being handed over to be crucified. So don't get discouraged as if you are less than because a spirit attacks you sometime.

- So now we can discern what is of God.
- We learned about positioning ourselves, and we learned that God will honor that positioning.
- And we learned about cleaning up our lives to have better flow, power, and authority walking in sonship. As He is, so are we in this world.
- Jesus was pure. So must we be.

FOUR

Chapter 4:
How God Speaks

Every way you can imagine.

He may **highlight** a side of a truck that has a **picture or word**. A clock that has certain numbers that have meanings. **A knock** in the middle of the night on a door that you open and no one is there. **A dog barking** in your room when you don't own a dog. **Angels** that speak, sing, dance. Confirmation through a **word someone else wrote.** **A movie** where he shows you the parable of the plot is a spiritual statement he is making (Good examples are Snow White and the Huntsman and The Matrix movies). **A dream.** Sometimes this includes going back in time in a dream. **A vision. Traveling in the spirit.** Many of us go to places, other countries, or go to heaven through ascending. I just went to Japan yesterday and with the cloud of witnesses and the Lord chose a lady who will be like a Billy Graham over the nation of Japan. I was told this lady's name and we imparted things into her life. We have gone to other nations doing work for the Lord in the spirit. Others have gone to help people, pray for them, ushering them into heaven. This is more common now than ever these days. **A scent.** Some of us have smelled spices and flowers—roses and cinnamon and other things. **A sound.** I hear my angels speaking audibly or knocking on a door in the middle of the night. **A sensing.** My daughter would hear them praying all night in my room while I slept. **A knowing. A feeling.** It can be a swoosh of an emotion, of love or bliss or ecstasy. **Love surges** where you want to tell everyone you love them. **A pressure or a pain as a word of knowledge**. **A picture** of someone's physical problem. **Through music.** Sometimes Jesus has come and moved in the music or danced in it, doing things in the song. That has happened many times where the Lord would use the song to show the saints and angels things. It's beyond what I can relate, but it is very awesome. Sometimes the Father would take a song and show angels things using the lyrics and at times I have taken music to use as intercession. You get stirred up in what it makes you think of and pray into that group of people, sending angels etc. It is so fun. **Worship, dance.** Angels dancing in the room or doing things in the music around me. Prophetic dance is being moved by the spirit, each move is a word and the words are seen and heard often by the angels. They may get information from your dance and be able to respond as a result. Sometimes they are moving the person in the prophetic dance and they are assigned to some individuals as a result to do prayer warfare through their dance.

They are able to ascend into heaven and see the throne room and dance as they see the Father. The Father moves their movements and brings that information to the earth through that dance. **The cloud of witnesses** come into the meetings; often they dance and worship with you in conferences. Jesus loves the drums and will do much with that beat when it is a drum roll. Being **an oracle or hearing one.** (where God uses your mouth to speak, and often the person who is being used has no idea what the next word to come out of their mouth will be) **Prophecy**, where the person senses or hears what they are about to say and says it as they sense and hear it. Also by things that become **lined up in place**, such as one thing just leads to another and things fall into place and at times land in your lap unexpected. Often when this happens, we look back and scratch our heads, wondering how this happened. **Through nature.** Some have heard the flowers speak. Sometimes a voice is a wind. Sometimes thunder. God spoke to me in thunder one time. It lasted about an hour, one word after another in the thunder he spoke to me. **Through signs and wonders. Gems, gold dust, gold in the teeth, manna**—although these are common for many. God is going to do more than this in the future. He has shown me that books will appear on people's shelves that were not there before. Even crazy things like your favorite ice cream you use to love and they don't make it anymore will suddenly appear in your refrigerator. Don't think that's odd. God has multiplied food for Heidi Baker many times, even Patricia King. And if you can believe it, God multiplied chocolate bars for Heidi.

So God is going to release some incredible fun things. Also, I have seen manna falling on people after they could not buy or sell because they did not have the mark of the beast as stated in book of revelations. **It was a dream I had.** I saw a man in Russia walking in the forest. He came upon two other men sitting at a picnic table, but it was winter and snow was all around. The man sat down and began to speak in Russian. I don't speak Russian so I don't know what they were saying. But soon after he began to speak, manna started to fall all around them. It seemed God guided this man there.

FIVE

Chapter 5:
Relationship

The Father's name means, "breath that gives life." Yod Hey Vav Hey. YHVH. The four faces of God. So when we are in him, we draw from him as the source of all our needs, the supply of everything you can imagine. Even emotions and feelings and needs of every kind shape and size. And He is everywhere. I like what Ian says when he points out, "What we focus on we multiply and what we focus on we empower. We give it our road in, if you will."

When you read Psalm One:
Psalm 1

1 Blessed is the one who does not walk in step with the wickedor stand in the way that sinners takeor sit in the company of mockers,
Here we see we are to separate ourselves from the world, including what we listen to and feed on.

2 but whose delight is in the law of the Lord, and who meditates on his law day and night.
You can choose to delight in the Lord, by thinking about everything that he created that is so awesome. Just look at nature and animals, horses, and lions and the sky and the mountains, and go 'wow'. You can say, "Lord, you're so amazing and beautiful and incredible and clever and wise, and of all the things in the world, you are the maker of them all. You created the brain and the mind and beauty and you are love and all these things. You are in all these things. There is no one like you. "And this says, "**Delight in the law of the Lord. His law is the word of God.**" So Jesus said not one jot or tittle will disappear

until all is fulfilled. So if the law is the whole word of God, and Jesus is the word, you can think of this scripture like this: **"but whose delight is Jesus and on Jesus he meditates (thinks about, dwells on loves on) on Jesus day and night."**

3 **That person is like a tree planted by streams of water,which yields its fruit in seasonand whose leaf does not wither—whatever they do prospers.** So we are planted next to the living waters. We are standing next to the living life source because we choose to draw nigh to him. He then draws near to us. And as a result we bear fruit. Jesus said, "I have called you to bear fruit, fruit that will last." It comes from relationship of practicing his presence by meditating, communing with and thinking about loving on Jesus. Your tree, because you are tucked under his wing, will not die or wither or see decay. No way! It's standing under the wing of the giver of life. He will not destroy his own. And as a result of being hidden under his wing, and even under his arm, close to his heart, whatever you do will prosper because it's him with you. He is doing it with you. As a result, it can't wither but will prosper. If you think of your dad and you out in his workshop, and you're building something together. Your dad knows what he is doing. You're helping, but it's more about being with your dad. He is overseeing the whole process. If something isn't right, he will fix it, right?

4 Not so the wicked! They are like chaff that the wind blows away.
5 Therefore the wicked will not stand in the judgment, nor sinners in the assembly of the righteous.
And we will stand in the judgment and we will stand in the assembly of the righteous (or out in the garage doing what dad and son do together). Those who are not connected to God can't even do any of these things, because they are disconnected from their life source! The one who oversees the project and does it with you. He teaches and guides you. Otherwise how can you start a project you know nothing about? Such are the wicked who refuse "dad time", who refuse meditating and communing with the one who was crucified for them.

They have idols of the heart, and are called harlots. That sounds rash, but its in the bible. He is jealous after you. Naturally He is. He deserves you, and you, <u>His way</u>. Not yours. Amen?

6 For the Lord watches over the way of the righteous, but the way of the wicked leads to destruction.
And so we have it here. He watches over us, but He is a part of it. The major part, and we love every moment of it. We love spending time with dad. He is the best dad in the whole universe, and Jesus is our best friend, brother and king. They are our family.

So why did I go into all that? Again, the Father loves, yearns for you, and so Jesus desires to spend time with you. He loves you, and because all the seeing, hearing and perceiving comes from this very thing—relationship.

Seek him with all your heart and he will give you the desires of your heart. So when He causes you to see, hear and perceive, it will be the best ever because it is to enhance your relationship.

SIX

Chapter 6:
Exercise Practice

For those who want to begin to hear and see and sense God, practice, patience and perseverance are keys. So as we spoke before about positioning, I want you to do an exercise. Part of learning is practice. Always go with the first thing that comes to your mind. That is the positioning part, and God will honor that, like positioning to catch the ball as stated earlier.

Prayer

"Father, I give myself permission to receive revelation and for you to grant me revelation now, in Jesus' name." Please forgive me for any time that my generational line or I did not believe or spoke against any of the gifts of the Holy Spirit in any way shape or form. Amen

If you get anything that is from the enemy, then deal with that. How? Ask the Father what it is related to and repent for that thing. Clear it out and go back to the first exercise again.

One word about "in Jesus' name."
I love the Ekklesia now shifts your mind about "in the name" of Jesus When we are walking with Jesus we are in him and he is in us. So you can think of being in him, or stepping into his name—stepping into Jesus. However it is also about carrying His signet ring of authority, that we are doing things because we are His ambassadors. We are sent by Him and walk in His behalf – not our own. So the key is to know His heart on a matter and walk into situations on His behalf… sent by Him. Then you can use His name, not your own name, not your own will… but His be done- using His name. We do not, use his name without walking in and with Jesus. That is why the sons of Sceva (Act 19) were beaten up trying to use the name of Jesus. But it is about stepping into relationship with Jesus and operating out of that relationship. He is closer than your brother. Closer than your breath. You are in him and he is in you, so you are drawing from him, the life source.

As stated earlier, the best way to ascend is through relationship. How do you form a relationship?
   1) Time with the one who loves you.
   2) Listening to him.
   3) Reading about him.
   4) Praying to him.
   5) Worship.
   6) Waiting on him.
   7) Seeking him with your heart in the desperate cry of your heart.
   8) Giving your all to him. Lay it down. Lay yourself down.
   9) Rest in him.

Then you can begin to step in by faith and do so daily through the blood of Christ as Jesus is the door in. Through relationship you become green with abundance of life and truth and loving him more. The more we love him, the more we love him. The more we seek him, the more we love him. We go from glory to glory.

Exercise

Close your eyes and imagine yourself on a pathway. On the way to the pathway on the grass, you see a doe, and the doe is running down the pathway to show you the way. You begin to follow and along the way there is a bench. You sit there and face the sun shining and a beautiful lake before you. Then Jesus sits down besides you. Now quietly listen and hear what he has to say to you. Remember Jesus is love. Write down what you are sensing, hearing, and what is being revealed.

Exercise

Think of one person in your family. Close your eyes. Now, ask the Lord, "Lord, what is one thing you can tell me about this person that if I were to speak to them today you would want them to know?" What is the first thing that comes to your mind? Write that down.

Exercise

Close your eyes.
Think of another person and ask the Lord to give you a picture of something for that person. What is the first thing that comes to your mind? Write it down. Your picture may be an impression or a sensing, a picture that is vague. Or it could be very clear to you.

So you might have a small picture or a word or two. The more you practice, the more you will get.

If you get nothing at all then pray this prayer and ask again. So it will go like this:
1) "Father, I give myself permission to receive revelation now, in Jesus' name."

2) "Father, what is one thing you can tell me about _____ that you want them to know?"

3) "Father, what is one picture you can show me about _____ that you want them to know?"

After you write this down for that person, go to them and say, "I am practicing seeing, hearing and perceiving. Can I give you what the Lord gave me for you?" If they say yes, say what you got for them. Then ask them, "Does this make any sense to you?"

Try to get feedback. Often times with feedback, you develop self-confidence. For example, a person may say, "Hey, I was just asking the Lord about that yesterday." Or, "Wow, I just was wondering about that very thing." Sometimes they may say that, and maybe not. If not, just know that if it is good, it is from him. Because you're positioning yourself for revelation again, he will honor that. Every good and perfect gift comes down from the Father of heavenly light.

Now let's try this again, only let's do perceiving. We are doing this because we want to begin to pay attention to our inner self, or our bodies. For example, if you ask that same question and you suddenly get a pain in your foot, you may be getting a revelation that that person needs healing in their foot. And you can write that down and pray for them. Then again, go to them and ask.

1) "Father, please give me a perception—a sensing, a feeling—about _____, that they would be benefited by me sensing or feeling what you will give."

You might perceive a healing, or you may sense that they need to deal with something you can pray for. Never give the negative to a person, but rather say, "I prayed for you regarding something that's bugging you or you are dealing with, as the Lord gave me indication to uplift you in prayer."

There are exceptions to this, but it's for another day.

Never give a word to someone that is negative. It should always be uplifting, encouraging and positive. Always turn the negative into a positive. Never share with anyone what you get for someone else. Integrity is very important. God will begin to trust you with things that you will not share. Also never gossip about another or speak negatively about anyone. Let God deal with that. On the other hand we are learning here and we just need to make adjustments where necessary. If you get a negative word, like, "I see a lot of snakes around a person's neck," you may pray, "Father, I take the sword of the spirit and cut off all those snakes in Jesus' name." Don't tell the person. Again, there are exceptions that will be for another time.

A word about prophecy and prayer and seeing for others.

God rarely shares negatives with people unless:
1) They are close to you in relationship.
2) You are in constant intercession for them and the Lord wants to let you know how to pray.
3) They are not listening to God themselves. He will tell them, if they don't listen he will start with a close person who hears from the Lord.
4) If you are beginning to learn discernment as a gift, you never, ever go to anyone and talk about it. It is for intercession purposes only.
5) If you are in a relationship with them, you can share if the Lord leads. For example, if I get a dream about my daughter regarding her daughter, I may say what that dream was or what the Lord is speaking. If your family member is in a good relationship with you, they will receive it; if not, perhaps you may plant a seed for them to think about, at the least. All dreams and such should be for their instruction or edification. In other words, the purpose is for life and if need be, a change.
6) Sometimes people will give you permission to speak into their lives because you are in relationship and you trust them. If that is the case, then it's ok. But they will tell you this.
7) Never intercede to hear or perceive in a long deep process of intercession and prophecy for someone unless you get their permission. Often this is caused many troubles because people peer into other people's lives without asking and come up with

personal things, and if you are not in a close, trusting relationship with that person, it becomes invasive.

8) You can give short words of encouragement from time to time If they are open to that, you can continue if they trust you.

9) Its not wise to give words for people you don't know unless you are in the spirit connected by them through other means. Such as a group. Say things like I am sensing. Don't say 'thus saith the Lord" be gentle with your approach. I will give positive short words to acquaintances but nothing too personal Its usually because they are in need of this word and welcome it. Things like, baby, husbands and moving are dangerous – to be taken in the wrong way. Please refrain from this unless you are a hired prophetic intercessor with a proven track record.

10) Never, ever travel in the spirit to another person's home, for words or anything, without permission from Jesus and his leading you or taking you, or you have been authorized to pray and prophesy for them. Of course over a nation, town situation is ok as you travel in the spirit for intercession after you have gone up, or are in courts etc.

11) Always ask God to put up a crew of angels with wings around you to protect you so that no one can invade your privacy, in the name of praying for them.

12) Stepping into heaven by faith for a person is fine and recommended more than anything else. Again, ask for permission. Even praying for someone without having cleaned up your own DNA can cause problems. How? Praying wrong. Again the negatives.

SEVEN

Chapter 7:
Seeing

Now let's look at seeing in the spirit. In this exercise, you can see how easy it is to see in the spirit, meaning moving pictures, or panoramic, seeing heaven, and angels etc.

Imagination

Imagination is a movie screen. Remember how they used to call it the 'silver screen'? So your imagination is a silver screen. It is not white, or black, so it can pick up all colors. The movie camera places those pictures onto the screen. Your pineal gland is like that. However, it goes deeper than that for those who have been filled up with the Holy Spirit. The screen isn't a flat screen to you, but a portal. It is a door. Remember, Jesus said, "I am the door," and his sheep go in (through that door) and go out (through him as the door) and find pasture. Pasture is a place of open land over which livestock may roam and feed. So if you are his sheep, you can find places to feed. Eat. What does that mean? Well, you know the word of God is food for the soul. We have that in print form. So when we go in and out of the door, we are finding new food of revelation. He is the bread that comes down from heaven. The hidden manna is through him. Don't think that, because we have the Bible, the door, which is Jesus, is closed. Remember that He is the door. And the point is to be fed with new manna, the food of heaven. So He speaks and imparts to us life. Why did Jesus say when He was with the woman at the well, "I have food to eat that you know not of?" That food was the hidden manna of revelation He gets directly from the Father. That is how he knew how many husbands that woman had and the one she was now with was not her husband. That manna from heaven gave Jesus much delight and it was his life source. Her saying, "When the Messiah comes, He will teach us all things," then Him saying, "I who is before you am He," was a joyful announcement of truth and His delightful food. So you, too, can get the manna from heaven that brings you life, that brings you such joy you will proclaim, "Oh, God is so good!" Jesus said this more than once but was not recorded. Our food from heaven is doing the Fathers will. Its also anything of the Holy Spirit. It gives life and light, and the FRUIT of the Holy Spirit is food indeed. The gifts of the spirit can produce the fruit if we use them in the right way.

Let's start where you are at:

Exercise

Close your eyes.

Now in your imagination to build your confidence, as you sit there, wherever you are, using the screen/portal/door of your imagination, w are going to go through the blood of Jesus, the door of revelation, and step into your hallway, or the place right outside of the room you are in. You are going to walk to your kitchen, then go to the refrigerator. You're going to take one thing to drink out of the refrigerator and put it on the counter, and then you're going to get a cup and put it down and pour that drink. You're going to put that drink container back into the refrigerator and take the cup and go sit down at the table. When you are at the table, taste that drink. What does it taste like? Do you feel the cold liquid in your mouth as you drink it? Drink it down now. Then get up from the table and go to your door, open it, step out, close the door behind you, and now take a slow walk outside. Walk slowly around your home. Look at every window around your home. Look at the trees, bushes, grass, flowers, or snow, depending on the season. Do you have a chair outside? Sit in that chair. Or sit on the porch. Sit there and imagine Jesus walking right up to you and sitting down next to you on the steps or in a new chair that just appeared if you did not have one.

As you sit with Jesus, say, "Jesus, hi. I love you thank you for spending time with me. What do you want to say to me?" Now be very quiet and listen to his voice, or listen to an impression inside your spirit. Let him take your hand and say what he wants to. Next, you stand up with Jesus and he embraces you. Then he starts to walk away and goes up into heaven again.

I would have you walk back into the house and come back into your room and come back to where you are now reading this. Or else you can just open your eyes as we go places by the speed of thought. You write it all down.

EIGHT

Chapter 8:
Ascending

A New Name

Years ago, I had very unusual things occur and in that time the Lord
would continue to call me Sarahboni. I realized that was my name to
Him. Its common amongst those who listen to Ian Clayton and
likeminded people that getting a new name from the Lord brings you
access in through the garden of Eden which had been closed after the
fall. Access to the garden is a wonderful experience. I had wonderful
time where we would be eating from the tree of life and seeing the life
that was there. You can go there too! Ask the Lord for your new name.
Paul use to be Saul. Abraham was Abram, and so on, so you too can be
renamed by the Lord. Just ask. Then add going to the garden as part of
your journeys .

Because Jesus said, "What you think in your heart is already done,"
what you think in your mind is done. Even using your imagination. It
is as if you did it with body and soul and spirit as much as if you did it
in spirit. I realized after going to places that it really really existed.
This was not made up! God will confirm this to you as you continue
on this path. Count on that!

Now how does this work?

The Holy Spirit, God, is everywhere.
So as I stated earlier, if you can imagine the Spirit of God is
everywhere, your spirit can go everywhere the Holy Spirit is. When
your spirit steps out of your body, it is in the midst of God who is
everywhere. We as a group often step in through the veil that Jesus
has torn. We step through the door which is Jesus and up Jacob's

ladder, and ascend up. I often see the threshold of heaven as a blue sapphire stone with gold and maybe white streaks in it. You start by using imagination. Imagination has the word "image" in it. So an image you think of is sanctified by laying oneself down as a living sacrifice and by prayer. We pray, "Father, I sanctify my imagination for your glory and for your goodness. I give every member of myself to you. Purge me with fire, the fire that will purge the dross and give me the passion for you in that purging fire."

As we ascend, we will speak out what we see. Sometimes ascending includes worship and praise to the Lord. Each person can participate in the ascension, speaking in turn what they see. Sometimes, as we ascend into heaven, we go places in heaven. Other times we ascend and end up in other countries where we release the glory of the Lord, or ask the Father to choose key people for ministry. We ask the Lord to bring out prophets, teachers, ministers, and evangelists. We pray for salvation over nations and sometimes we land in the nation and release things.

There are rules for your sake that are set up for this, though. These are safety rules of the road in life.

The rules are:
1) Never go here and there in the world unless you are taken by God. How do you know you are taken? Well, you didn't sit and plan on going here or there, but you find yourself here or there because you're on a mission in intercession and you know God is with you in it as he instructs you in that mission. It is not something you sat and planned and decide on yourself. Sometimes He just takes you spontaneously. (I have gone up and sat at the threshold of heaven and asked to descend into a place – getting permission first before. Once I ascended with another person and they went to a planet and they were describing it to me, I wanted to go and see but the Father said, no, stay here, this is his. So all the while he was describing what he was seeing, I was up in the clouds in heaven facing the direction of the planet he was on. Now I also go to planets and explore.

2) Go up to heaven by using your imagination, seeing stairs on purpose or a portal. The point is, you're going home to daddy's house. So you go and worship or pray and praise and see what God has to say to you.
3) Never go and engage the enemy on purpose unless you are in intercession and are advanced in your training regarding this.

Portals in the word:

Now take your bible. Open it up to Matthew 5, verse 1 "Now when Jesus saw the crowds, he went up on a mountainside and sat down. His disciples came to him, 2 and he began to teach them."

There are many portals in the word of God. This is one. So as you read this scripture, place yourself in that picture. Jesus walked up a mountainside. So start at the beginning of the mountainside. Jesus begins to walk up that mountain; where are you? Why not walk along side of him? Who knows how long the walk is, but let's say five or ten minutes.

So as you walk and talk with him, what will you ask? What would he say in response? Listening is very, very important. Take every impression, every thought into consideration. You are giving Jesus room to talk to you. You may not want to say one word, so just listen. He knows it all already, so listening is an extremely important part of being in relationship with the Lord and seeing.

Notice His sandals, clothing, color of his hair, the day—is it sunny out? Look at the rocks on the mountainside, the grass, and the flowers. As you finally get to the top, the next part was that the disciples followed him. So they come in behind, and they sit down with you and him. Then the next part is He begins to teach. Watch his mouth speaking. Listen to his voice, His eyes, His tone of His voice. Glance at the people. Practice this in your mind's eye; see the images on the screen inside your mind. You will begin to see how you're not imagining anything anymore, but rather having a vision or encounter.

He opens his mouth and says:

3

"Blessed are the poor in spirit,for theirs is the kingdom of heaven.
4

Blessed are those who mourn,for they will be comforted.
5

Blessed are the meek, for they will inherit the earth.
6

Blessed are those who hunger and thirst for righteousness,for they will be filled.
7

Blessed are the merciful,for they will be shown mercy.
8

Blessed are the pure in heart,for they will see God.
9

Blessed are the peacemakers,for they will be called children of God.
10

Blessed are those who are persecuted because of righteousness,for theirs is the kingdom of heaven.
11 Blessed are you when people insult you, persecute you and falsely say all kinds of evil against you because of me. 12 Rejoice and be glad, because great is your reward in heaven, for in the same way they persecuted the prophets who were before you."

So as you sit with him on the mountain, what does He turn and say to you? Are you listening? You might get an impression, a sense, a feeling, and a picture. You might see His mouth move or not.

Now you have an angel on the right side of you standing there. What does he look like? What colors is his wearing? Ask him his name and his purpose for being there. As we practice, we begin to engage, or commune with, heaven and the kingdom of heaven on the earth.

Father, open up the reader's eyes to see what is going on around them in the spirit.

Angel Exercise

Close your eyes and ask the Lord, "Lord, give me a sense of what is around me and where my angels are in this room. Father, tell me what purpose they have for being here."

It starts with little small acts of faith and engagement. You can be living in this day after day.

Often when we ascend into heaven, we start with something small. We talked about this with a group; now let's see if you can do this yourself. We step through the veil, through the blood of Yeshua, our door. We ascend Jacob's ladder, and then you might see a spiral ladder going up into heaven. It may be blue, or all types of colors. What is on the stairs? You might see roses on the stairs. What is around it? You might see clouds, birds, light, or color. Do you see angels there to guide your way? As you ascend, what happens next? Sit wait on the Lord and see. Because this is so important, God wants you to connect with heaven and grow in this, that He will assist you. Ask for angels to come and help you ascend.

Prayer:
Father, we thank you for this gift and it is for a very special purpose for your body, for the Ekklesia. We know you want us to function in heaven and bring it to earth. You want us to grow quickly as a result of ascending up into heaven. So we ask for your assistance now in Jesus name. Thank you Lord. We invite Holy Spirit to fill us up and journey with us. Amen.

Intercession Exercise

Jesus wants us to pray and intercede from heaven. So by faith, step into the heaven through the blood of Jesus and the door who he is. Step in and stand at the threshold of heaven, the clouds are around, the blue sapphire stone floor and begin to worship, praise, thanksgiving and then petition. Often times then the Lord may lead you in closer to Him. He may extend his scepter. You may see Him and He will fulfill your dreams by telling you things about what your future holds. He has all your scrolls for you to engage with. He may ask you to wait there and see what He has for you. So intercession is part of the ascending. It isn't always of course but God wants you up there! Trust me on this one!

Exercise

Practice ascending:

Close your eyes and picture a veil or a drapery. Step through it and say, "Father, I step through the veil by the blood of Jesus and I step into and through Jesus who is the door. Father, I ascend up into your kingdom through a portal or a door or a stairway, which ever you choose." You can ask the Father, "May I proceed?" He always says yes, but you can do this to know you are welcome. "Father. I land my feet on the threshold of heaven." As stated earlier, I always see a dark blue marble-sapphire flooring with gold streaks in it. It feels cool, perhaps, slick beneath your feet. See the angel standing there on your right? Say, "Father, I step into your kingdom of heaven to connect with heaven to learn about you, to learn about heaven, to bring heaven down. To learn how to grow and to connect with you. So, Father, where would you like to take me?"

Right now you may see yourself walking forward. There are low laying clouds all around, and he says, "Come here and kneel. I want to commission you as a son."
He may place a crown on your head and knight you, giving you a scroll of sonship. He may say, "All I have is yours. I welcome you as a son. I give you the name _____, which means _____. Come, I will show you the glory of my kingdom."
Right now I see a waterfall that has fire in it, and glory and red. Red is the spirit of the Lord, It comes right out of his heart, the glory of the Lord and his goodness. Colors of the rainbow and bright light all around.

Keep engaging until you feel you are to pull out. But the truth is, if you push yourself to look and engage, you will see more and engage more. Write out what you see. I see a red mantle given to those who attend this vision, and a sword to learn to fight the good fight of your faith, through the blood of Jesus and the word of God, the word of your testimony. It is written in heaven. God will make you a well-watered garden so that you are able to take on the giants and bring others into the kingdom of sonship and ascending. He is with you; do not be afraid. Rest and be assured. God will bring things into the known that is unknown and He will bring glory to his name through this visitation in the heavenly realm.

As I write this, I see an angel reading and speaking this from a scroll. Even now a scroll of remembrance for all those who enter in. God wants you to plunder heaven because it never runs dry. He celebrates his loved ones with his provision.

Thank you, Lord. We honor you, Yeshua and Father. Thank you that, without you, we can do nothing. Thank you for saying yes and redeeming us. We honor what you did on the cross and all that you submitted yourself to with the Father. Amen.

NINE

Chapter 9:
Leaning on Your Beloved

Intimacy is pressing in and knowing the Lord as a personal friend and love. To know him is to love him even more. The door in is faith. As you believe, so it is. He has a special and different relationship with each of us. He wants to see himself in you. I use to hear him say, "I love myself in you. "Or, "I love to see me in you." God wants to spend time with you on a daily basis. Worship him. Press in to him, crave and lean on him, draw nigh to him and he will draw nigh to you. I can't say enough about repentance, cleansing your DNA and cleansing your bloodline. This helps you in your seeing and ascending process.

God will show you more about this if you ask him. But when you get saved, all the things you suffered with don't just disappear. Someone needs to say "sorry" to God. Right? If your child went and hit your neighbor, wouldn't you say 'sorry for your child if they were too young to understand? If your dog bit your friend, wouldn't you say sorry to your friend? It's the same when we ask for forgiveness from the Lord on our generational stuff—what our forefathers did against God. We are disagreeing with it, we are saying, "We divorce ourselve from this. We want no part of this. We do not stand and walk with this sin." Then God cleanses it from us. He is that good.

There were gifts imparted to your generations that were held up because of sin. When you repent, you offer a way for those gifts to be passed down to you and your children and children's children. If you honor God, he will honor you.

A small group and me met every single day, Monday through Friday for one hour, and we worship, ascend, and do all kinds of things in the spirit, including going to other planets and other nations. We repent fo sins of our children and ourselves. We intercede over the world. We worship and praise him and sing to him in tongues, often getting an interpretation, then God pours down on us incredible blessing. One blessing he gave us all one day, was that our generations after us will be blessed. He said, "Doctors will come, scientists, musicians, astronomers, and botanists. Some studying things from the safari in Africa the animals on a whole new playing field, learning never before known things," and so on. They would be people who were really good at many different things. They would excel and be a blessing. They will be walking with God. Our little group was just that, none of us were wealthy and we all come from broken backgrounds, from many divorces and illnesses and crippled. But through prayer DNA cleansing, and deliverance, we are walking in complete freedom on many levels. One day, during our daily gathering to worship and spend time the God our Father and Jesus, he said, "Guess what? I am going to bless your generations after you because you are faithful and come together to meet with me day after day." We were very encouraged and amazed at his goodness. During this time, we have many visits from angels and the cloud of witnesses. They come and pray with us, interceding and helping us on our missions. There was a day none of us could see or engage. Now we do so daily. So take heart. Start and keep doing it. Keep pursuing the Lord and meeting with him.

Quest to Walk with God 1 & 2, series by Neville Johnson, is also a great way to encourage you as you learn to wait on the Lord and expect things to happen.

We are called to transform the universe by turning it back to God's original creation before the fall, and we do this by ascending into heaven.

TEN

Chapter 10:
Being Sensitive

As the spirit of the Lord falls, you begin to sense things. It is the same if you had your eyes closed, and you felt a feather fall on your arm. You would feel that. The same is with the sensing and the feeling of the spirit. A sensing or a feeling that impresses you. You begin to feel this and know that even a slight picture or a sense that you begin to feel that and know what God is saying. You begin to listen to your body and you're sensing things within your heart, your spirit. So filling up with the spirit of the Lord is highly important. You may get bugged by the flesh and you can also sense who is not being sensitive or walking in the spirit. When the Holy Spirit is in you and you are filled up and are sensitive, it's as if the Lord can gently drive your spirit in one direction or the other. For example Jesus was 'led by the spirit' to go into the wilderness for His 40 day fast.

Often times you don't want talking because it breaks the spirits flow. You begin to feel that and it takes a lot of patience to wait on the person who is talking and to get back in the flow of Holy Spirit. One way to get more sensitive is to fast and also to worship, to press in and ask for more and more impartation of the Holy Spirit, hosting his presence by keeping pure in heart, mind and body, to listen to His spirit and act on what he says. The Lord is going to outgrow many people from their current positions and bring an alignment and unity together in other places. God never wants you to put a cap on how far you can go. Religion and control will box you in and keep you under wraps while the Father will lead those who are hungry into greener pastures and territory. He will do this by gathering them online or through other means.

Being sensitive to his call is very important. This may come as prompting; don't argue with it, but heed the call and run after him. Don't delay. Don't wait for a stubborn husband or wife to get on board. Some of us may desire to run toward the Lord and untangle ourselves from anything holding us back by making Him our first love

This is from Frances Metcalf's book:

Our lover appeared again unto me and these were his words unto me: "Speak unto my loves in the earth and tell them to set their lamp burning brightly, for soon shall I send my chariots in the dark of the night to gather them to the great wedding feast I am preparing. Many have been bidden, but few have made themselves fully ready to appear before the hosts of heaven attired in bridal array. The nuptial feast is ordered. I have sought throughout the centuries for my lovers. I have found many servants and friends, some disciples and countless believers; but I have found few true lovers who will rise and run after me with a passion that responds to my own burning heart of love. I offer my Father-Mother heart of love to all my children, and they flee to my arms and abide under my shadow; but few, oh, so few, rise to receive the embrace of my bosom. Few partake of the creative love which is the heart throb of the universe—the fiery center of the cosmos. Yea, I have found few mortals who thirst for this inebriating wine enough to quaff it freely, for there is death as well as life within the cup. All other loves must be sacrificed and consumed in the path of my flaming steps. And so I call and call, and my cry is unheeded by the sons of men. O, come up, come up, you few who will venture out of the beaten paths of the lowlands; come up into the highway (the more excellent way) that leads you up, up, up into the hidden recesses of the mount that cannot be touched by flesh—the mount of the one who is a consuming fire. I call, and I long, and I wait for the day when I shall find my heart's desire, my true bride—for the day of my marriage tarries long and I wait with yearning." Maloney, James (2012-04-30). Ladies of Gold, Volume 2: The Remarkable Ministry of the Golden Candlestick . WestBowPress. Kindle Edition used by permission.

ELEVEN

Chapter 11:
Group Ascending

As stated before, part of the order of Melchizedek which is the four faces of God is the oracle, the prophetic eagle. An oracle is the same as if you allowed the Lord to use your mouth. You sit back and allow the Lord to move on your mouth, resting the same as if you were to speak in tongues. Some of us know that two of the faces are the priest and the king. The priest steps in and worships the Lord before the arc of the covenant. The king decrees and declares. The ox is the apostleship or the legislation, working in the courts of heaven as well as doing the administration part of the four faces, plowing ground. Many of us ascend and gain more of what God wants to say to us through these and other things of heaven.

While I run The Rev group, we ascend together. Some of us have a small group who meet together privately, and then there are our mentoring sessions that are a bit more public. As said before, getting the junk out of our lives is a process that will help you a great deal. When you decide to ascend with a few people, it's best to have at least three. We have had four and five before. When you get with these people, you have to make an honest commitment to stick it out. The enemy will tell you lies about yourself, perhaps, but you must recognize that it is the enemy and ignore them, unless repentance is needed.

As you walk this out, you begin to get to know one another and flow begins to happen. There may be a time of adjustment. There are times we all just speak out what we are sensing; other times one may take the lead. Still other times we may sit in complete quiet, all the while being on the phone with each other, and God is showing us individual stuff while each one is quiet in his presence.

How do you find people? Ask the Lord to lead you to them. Also, get in a group of likeminded people by searching Facebook. Much has happened through Facebook through the years. Friends come and go, but God has built things using this social media that no one could possibly really know about completely. Many, many divine connections have occurred through it. It has changed, it seems, but many have settled as to where they are and where they are going to stay. There was a time of preparation and a time of adjusting, while the Lord had shaken out what is to remain. Those who have stayed with it have seen incredible personal growth. While new people come into the groups we have, acceleration and growth occurs. There is always a generation behind us we must prepare for. If you are looking for a group you can ask the Father if ours is the one for you. If not ask Him to lead and direct you regarding these things. I had found that those who are in the groups grow faster and they know we need one another. Those who don't belong to any group may find it hard to be alone while growing in these things. We need community. Thank you Jesus for providing this for us. You may find your own church may not be into these things, but you can try to introduce them to it. Some have chosen to just work with us in the groups and we are their church. However we are more than that, we are the Ekklesia, that works not just with one another but with the cloud of witnesses and the angels. They and the Lord of course are your true family.

Ascending's and Courts

During group ascensions one may lead and the others follow, and then each person takes turn on what they see. The lead person may start out like, we step in through the veil through the holy of holiness and ascend Father by Faith. We step in under the order of Melchizedeck. And then they may say… "I see this" . Then another person would say, I "see this" and the seeing would be part of the whole picture usually. When you go through the courts, it's the same thing. But you say, your stepping into the courts and then you begin the repentance. After you repent you can ask for papers of divorce that divorce yourself from the trading floor that is related to what you repented for. Then ask for the papers of justice. These are scrolls. You get them and put them in your mountain. Your mountain is your area of influence. When you are in the mobile court you can all take turns repenting as a group or you can do so by yourself. (mobile court in heaven is for personal repentance issues) During your court session you can call forth the accusers. Jesus will judge it and remove the issue from you. This may take more than one session. Again you can ascend by yourself and take note of what you are getting and see what the Lord is saying. You can return to that place because there is no time in heaven. All time is at one time.

The Ekklesia of the Most High has a book in heaven of the history of it, even a place that others will go into and see many things in that place.

God showed me this.

TWELVE

Chapter 12 :
Encounters with The Father, Jesus, the Cloud of Witnesses and The Angels

I am only speaking this to you so that you can see what is possible when you ascend. Doing that by faith through the veil, through the blood, Jesus is the door. This is some of what we had seen during ascending's. The other reality is that angels are all around you. You can purposely engage with them so you see and hear them often. Test the spirits – and know that heaven- heaven's realm is accessible all the

time. This is why you can live a lifestyle of heaven ascending and a lifestyle of being in heaven more than the earth. The reason is the angels are of heaven's realm and it is possible to engage with them on a constant basis. I do. So you can to. There is not a day that goes by that I do not hear, see and sense and commune with them.
In that realm, accessing heaven is much easier and often comes spontaneously as well as if I purpose my heart on it. So you can walk in that as well.

Here are some of the encounters I have had.
The Father has come and danced with me, or just came into the room and said, "I am your Father," and Jesus has been in our midst. He would be in my room while we ascended and of course the angel's. We have gone up golden staircases. We have gone to other parts of the world and chose people who would intercede, who would become ministers and teachers and evangelists. We have interceded for nations. We have gone into and over the White House. We have gone to other places in the universe, to other planets, and seen other creatures of creation. (I'll be writing about more of this in a book that will be about these mysteries)

We have done much repentance and DNA cleansing courts.
We have partnered with the cloud of witnesses, who show up and help bring intercession into specific places that were somehow their passion. One of my favorite times is when Hildegard Von Bingen came in and sprinkled cinnamon on our heads, and of course we had to look up the meaning of cinnamon.   We have gone to Catholic churches and prayed for new judgments. We have gone into the Holy of Holies and stepped through the veil as priests and kings.

We have gone to the mountain of the Father and sat with him on his lap. We have gone to the wine room and the treasury and countless other places. Some have been very intense, including the parts of the universes that were still in light, while others are in dark.

Jesus showed me that the universe is in layers and some of it is not yet created. He also showed me how it was a web held together in many dimensions. Once, while I was painting, I saw the angel that I was talking to. I had a few that day that were talking to one another while I was painting, and he just took a step forward and said, "like this," and it opened before him, the universe, and he could dash right off into it.

The Lord has many awesome things for us to see and experience. Once I was shown how you can be in many places at once. It's like looking into one room and another room as you stand in the middle of the wall of them both. Anywhere the Spirit of the Lord is, you can be, since where the spirit is, there is freedom and liberty.

On other occasions, I have seen many of the cloud. King Richard, Enoch, Elijah, Mary, Jesus's mother and John the Baptist—who loves to dance in conferences—as well as some of the people I would watch documentaries about. I would start to watch them and they would just show up, like Einstein, Isaac Newton, Galileo, and Augustine's mentor, the Bishop of Ambrose and St. Joseph of Cupertino, to name a few. Funny things have happened in these. Once my room was filled with the cloud to intercede for the new salvations coming on the new wave of the fire that we are all waiting for. All night they were praying chatting and having a party in my room. The clearest person I have seen and spoken to was Shem. I get visits from many various people often, and the Lord is always in their midst when this occurs. We are needing the Ekklesia of Heaven to connect with us, but also because they are our family. They love us.

I pray this will get you quickly on your journey, as it is the Lord's will that if you are reading this, it means you're hungry and are desiring and as a result are one of those who will tap into these things.

Father thank you for this reader. Asking you to give them the double of what they already carry of your presence and that as they have done the exercise's in this book that you would cause them to accelerate forward and as a result grow faster in heaven. Asking you also Father that they will know you more as a result and that they will delight themselves in you. Amen , Shalom, Selah and blessing.

GROW IN PASSION FOR HIM!

Job22: 12"Is not God in the height of heaven?And see the highest stars, how lofty they are!13 And you say, 'What does God know?Can He judge through the deep darkness?14 Thick clouds cover Him, so that He cannot see,And He walks above the circle of heaven.'15 Will you keep to the old wayWhich wicked men have trod,16 Who were cu down before their time,Whose foundations were swept away by a flood?17 They said to God, 'Depart from us!What can the Almighty do to them?' 18 Yet He filled their houses with good things;But the counsel of the wicked is far from me.19 "The righteous see it and are glad,And the innocent laugh at them:20 'Surely our adversaries are cu down,And the fire consumes their remnant.'21 "Now acquaint yoursel with Him, and be at peace;Thereby good will come to you.22 Receive. please, instruction from His mouth,And lay up His words in your heart.23 If you return to the Almighty, you will be built up;You will remove iniquity far from your tents.24 Then you will lay your gold in the dust,And the gold of Ophir among the stones of the brooks.25 Yes, the Almighty will be your gold And your precious silver;26 For then you will have your delight in the Almighty,And lift up your face to God.27 You will make your prayer to Him,He will hear you,And you will pay your vows.28 You will also declare a thing,And it will be established for you;So light will shine on your ways.29 When they cast you down, and you say, 'Exaltation will come!'Then He will save the humble person.30 He will even deliver one who is not innocent;Yes, he will be delivered by the purity of your hands."

END

About the Author
Paula S. MinGucci lives in a suburb of Chicago, IL
She works full time doing private ministry
and mentoring and training others.
Contact: www.theekklesiaofthemosthigh.com

11850714R00031

Made in the USA
Monee, IL
18 September 2019